TAO

TO KNOW & NOT BE KNOWING

EASTERN WISDOM

CHRONICLE BOOKS

SAN FRANCISCO

A Labyrinth Book

First published in the United States in 1993 by Chronicle Books.

Copyright © 1993 by Labyrinth Publishing (UK) Ltd.

Design by Meringue Management

The Little Wisdom Library–Eastern Wisdom was produced by Labyrinth
Publishing (UK) Ltd. Printed and bound in Singapore by Craft Print Pte. Ltd.

Library of Congress Cataloging in Publication Data: Tao, Eastern Wisdom.

p.   cm.   (Eastern Wisdom) Includes bibliographical references.

ISBN 0–8118–0420–8:

1. Taoism. I. Chronicle Books (Firm) II. Series.

BL1920.T257 1993

299. 514– – dc20   92–42256

                                                          CIP

Distributed in Canada by Raincoast Books,

112 East Third Avenue, Vancouver, B.C. V5T 1C8

10 9 8 7 6 5 4 3 2 1

Chronicle Books

275 Fifth Street, San Francisco, CA 94103

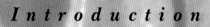

Introduction

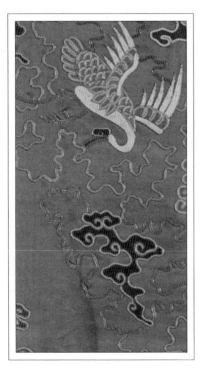

The short work you hold in your hands represents an honest attempt at providing a concise statement of the wisdom of Taoism. The *Tao Te Ching*, the most famous text of Taoism, has over the past century and a half become one of the world's most translated books, and has won admirers not only among the emperors of China but also among European thinkers such as Tolstoy and Heidegger. Far from being a collection of quaint apothegms, it is, in fact, a practical philosophy which has stood the test of time.

To many scholars, survival itself has seemed to be one of the major themes of Taoism, particularly a survival based on weakness rather than on strength. Despite the legend introduced here, which makes the author of the *Tao Te Ching* an older contemporary of

Confucius—a legend that is true to the very ancient roots of the work's philosophy and captures well the mood of disenchantment that lies behind it—we now tend to place the composition of the *Tao Te Ching* in a period in history of escalating violence that eventually produced the totalitarian First Emperor of China, master even in death of a host of terra-cotta warriors and unifier of the Chinese empire.

Its true author we will never know, for he or she took pains to hide behind an assumed identity. The earliest manuscripts of the *Tao Te Ching*, discovered two decades ago in China, show that within a generation of the First Emperor's death, China's rulers were being forced to take its ideas seriously, something that perhaps contributed to the longevity of the Chinese Imperial system despite the later displacement

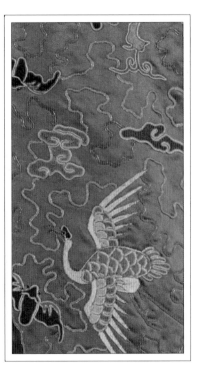

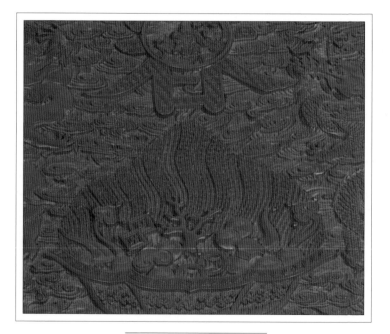

Previous pages, 10-11: Detail from the patterns of a
Chinese silk robe. *Above:* Detail from a red laquer,
peach–shaped box from the Ming Dynasty.

of Taoism by Confucian thought.

The lessons of Taoism, then, may be learned by the powerful or by the powerless, but it is the powerless who have always best heeded the message, whether the politician driven into distant exile or the peasant despairing of a more equitable society. How differently people, even in ancient China, understood the texts of Taoism comes as something of a surprise, for warriors might find strategy in them while Buddhists found intimations of their own developing way. Openness to interpretation, however, cannot be equated with shallowness of meaning; the Taoist way of thinking draws the reader in, seeking more.

The riches of the Taoist tradition are considerable. In addition to the many translations of the *Tao Te Ching*, readers may wish to go on to consult works such as the *Chuang Tzu* and the *Lieh Tzu*, both available in translations by Angus Graham, one of the greatest Western scholars of Chinese thought of our century. Even now a new generation of scholars is working to bring more of this remarkable tradition to light. The wisdom contained in this volume is what inspires their efforts.

T.H. Barrett
Professor of East Asian History
University of London

_=_

The Tao
The Formless Form

_=_

Tao is a single comprehensive symbol within the Chinese language. Its significance can be understood if we compare it to selecting one word in the English language and making that word one of the most meaningful above all others. The English language does not work in this way, but because of a philosophy, Taoism, the word and symbol of Tao, achieves this importance. Tao may be a path, a track, an idea or principle, a system or doctrine, an order. It may also formulate a matrix or structure—a kind of complete reality within the universe.

As with many of the other "Eastern" philosophies, such as Zen, the Tao is an experience rather than a "thought." It is essentially too comprehensive and all-embracing simply to be understood through a single mental expression, and is therefore difficult for the Western mind to interpret. It is the experience of the universal Way: the essential reality from which all resulting ways may be understood.

To fathom this reality, the Taoist philosophers concentrated their efforts on the well-being of individuals, the harmony available within social groups, and the methods by which consciousness could most readily be evolved. This trio was considered within the understanding of the Tao to be the three foundations of life.

Previous pages, 14-15: A two-handled jar from the Yuan Dynasty period. *Opposite:* A celadon and russet jade boulder depicting two monks ascending the steep path on a holy mountain site.

Lao Tzu
The Legend

here is a legend that on the fourteenth of September, 604 B.C., in the village of Ch'u Jen in the county of K'u, in the Kingdom of Ch'u in ancient China, a woman, leaning against a plum tree, gave birth to a child. Since it was known that this child was to be a great man—a god, no less—the circumstances of his birth were extraordinary. According to the legend, he had been conceived sixty-two years before, when his mother had admired a falling star, and after so many years in the womb, he was able to

> "Whosoever stands on tiptoe
> does not stand firmly.
> Whosoever stands with legs astride
> will not advance.
> Whosoever wants to shine
> will not be enlightened.
> Whosoever wants to be someone
> will not become resplendent.
> Whosoever glorifies himself..."

speak as soon as he was born. Pointing to the plum tree, he announced: "I take my surname from this tree." To the name Plum (Li in Chinese) he prefixed the word ear (Erh), his own being large, and so became Li Erh. However, since his hair was already snow-white, most people called him Lao-tzu, or Old Sir. Little is known about his youth. He spent his adult years in the Chinese Imperial capital at Loyang, first as Palace Secretary and then as Keeper of the Archives for the court of Chou.

Page 18: Lao-tzu left the capital of Loyang disillusioned with the decay of the Chou dynasty. Here he is portrayed traveling on his ox. *Overleaf, page 22:* A buffalo statuette splashed with turquoise gilt. *Page 23:* A Chinese drawing of Confucius, said to be Lao-tzu's adversary.

We are told that at the age of 160, Lao-tzu became disillusioned with the Chou dynasty and its evident decay, and resolved to pursue virtue in a more congenial atmosphere. Riding in a chariot drawn by a black ox, he left the Middle Kingdom through the Han-Ku Pass, which leads westward from Loyang. The Keeper of the Pass, Yin Hsi, who, from a reading of the state of the weather, had expected the arrival of a sage, addressed him as follows: "You are about to withdraw yourself from sight. I pray you to compose a book for me." Lao-tzu thereupon wrote the *Tao Te Ching*—The Sacred Book of the Tao and the Te, which was composed of five thousand Chinese

> ...does not accomplish works.
> Whosoever boasts of himself
> will not be exalted.
> For TAO he is like kitchen refuse and a festering sore.
> And all the creatures loathe him.
> Therefore: whosoever has TAO
> does not linger with these."

characters. After completing the book, he departed for the West. We do not know when or where he died.

The times in which Lao-tzu wrote his book were filled with political and social conflict. The difficulties are said to have begun in 711 B.C when the Chou dynasty was forced out of its capital city by barbarians from the northwest. The leaders of this once powerful dynasty were compelled to reestablish the capital of their kingdom 200 miles eastward in the city of Loyang. The decay of the eastern Chou, as the dynasty was called thereafter, continued for a total of 522 years. From being feudal monarchs, with the power to control their "vassals" or peasants, the rulers of Chou effectively became no more than impotent figureheads. As a result, the vassals began to rebel and make war, not against the barbarians, who pressed at the outer borders of their kingdom, but against one another. War led to more war, treachery to more treachery, until it seemed that the known world of China was to be reduced to a wasteland. The great sage, Confucius, dedicated his whole life to imposing a moral system in the hope of preventing further atrocities, but even at his death nothing had changed.

Lao-tzu's beliefs were in direct opposition to those of Confucius, his contemporary, for he believed that

Confucius had in part triggered the chaos and decline by preaching his code of morality. And it is here that we begin to see the "Way." Lao-tzu's method of enacting change, his answer to social and human chaos, was the doctrine of "inaction," or, in Chinese, *wu wei* (literally "not doing"), exposed in his book *Tao Te Ching*.

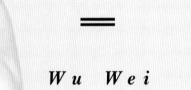

Wu   Wei

Lao-tzu proposed that the best way to cope with the "pillage, tyranny, slaughter," and the war-hunger of the lords was to do nothing at all. To suggest a theory of inaction in such circumstances would seem potentially dangerous. However, Lao-tzu's version of "inaction" is rather a special one and it provides the foundation of the Tao. The inaction he recommends finds the seat of its power within the individual and his or her understanding of the nature of all things.

"Such things [weapons of war] are wont to rebound."

"The more laws you make, the more thieves there will be."

"The Sage does not boast, therefore he is given credit."

"He who acts harms, he who grabs lets slip."

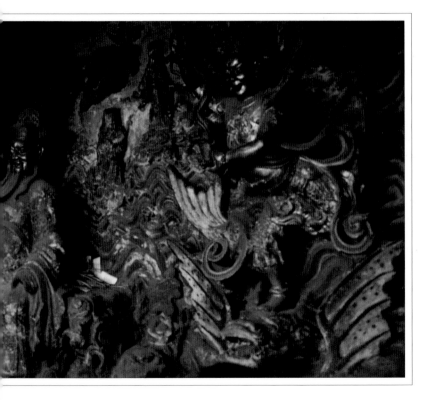

The principle underlying these four statements is that in human relationships, force defeats itself. Every action produces a reaction, every challenge a response. There is a law of inertia inherent in existence; the tendency is for every aspect of this existence to continue to be what it is. Interfere with its natural state and it resists, as a stone resists crushing. If it is a living creature it resists actively, as a wasp being crushed will sting.

The resistance to interference in relation to living creatures is unique, and evolution might be thought of as a march towards ever more highly articulated and effective resistance. Humans and human societies are as such highly responsive to challenge, and when anyone, ruler or subject, tries to *act* upon individual or collective humanity, the ultimate result is the

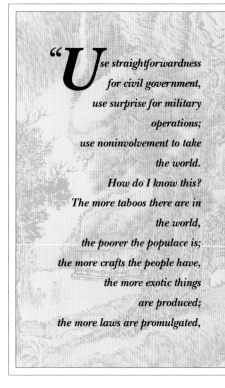

"*Use straightforwardness for civil government, use surprise for military operations; use noninvolvement to take the world.*

How do I know this? The more taboos there are in the world, the poorer the populace is; the more crafts the people have, the more exotic things are produced; the more laws are promulgated,

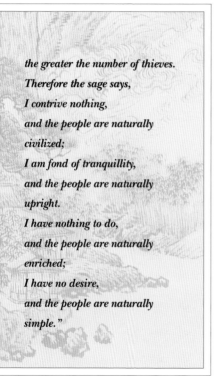

the greater the number of thieves.

Therefore the sage says,

I contrive nothing,

and the people are naturally

civilized;

I am fond of tranquillity,

and the people are naturally

upright.

I have nothing to do,

and the people are naturally

enriched;

I have no desire,

and the people are naturally

simple."

opposite of what is intended.

Lao-tzu asserts that challenges are to be ignored and that to deal with them by responding is the greatest of mistakes. In Lao-tzu's opinion there is no achievement through action. The only way is *wu wei*, "To yield is to be preserved whole..." *Wu wei* is the only means to achieve true success: sooner or later deliberate intervention always results in failure. One is thus almost forced into practicing non-doing.

Previous pages, 24–25: A statuette of Kuan-Ti, the Chinese God of War, who brings conflict to the world. *Pages 26-27*: Rock carving of Taoist divinity. *These pages, background image in box:* A drawing depicting a secluded Taoist monastery.

"Do nondoing,
strive for nonstriving,
savor the flavorless,
regard the small as important,
make much of little,
repay enmity with virtue;
plan for difficulty when
it is still easy,
do the great while it
is still small.
The most difficult
things in the world
must be done while
they are easy;
the greatest things in the
world
must be done while they are small."

It is important to understand that *wu wei* is not the same as nothingness and does not represent an ideal of absolute inaction. On the contrary, it is a particularly useful attitude since it makes all doing both possible and effective. *Wu wei* is the understanding of natural law—of that which already is—a law that if followed confers true strength and effectiveness on all action.

Above: A decorated plate. *Opposite:* An ivory statuette of the Taoist immortal Chung-li Ch'üan. *Overleaf, pages 32-33:* A panel of blue silk portraying a Taoist immortal attended by two servants bearing gourd vases.

The *Tao Te Ching* is founded upon a general principle which governs all existence and, at the same time, reverts back to the observing individual. This principle is called the Tao, or the Way. The true Tao is at once the formless, nameless Principle of the Universe, the art of living that consists of letting nature alone, of not intervening in the course of events; an art that has its applications as much in the life of the individual (long life, spirituality) as in politics (letting people live freely and in peace). The *Tao Te Ching* is not a philosophical treatise. It contains no demonstrations of any kind; it gives only conclusions, not the steps by which they are reached.

It is up to each individual to take the steps on his own. The truth is already instinctively known by each one of us as the ultimate law that governs existence. And true virtue, *Te*, in Chinese, is the ability to recognize and follow the Way. Literally translated the *Tao Te Ching* is: the Way; Virtue; and Book.

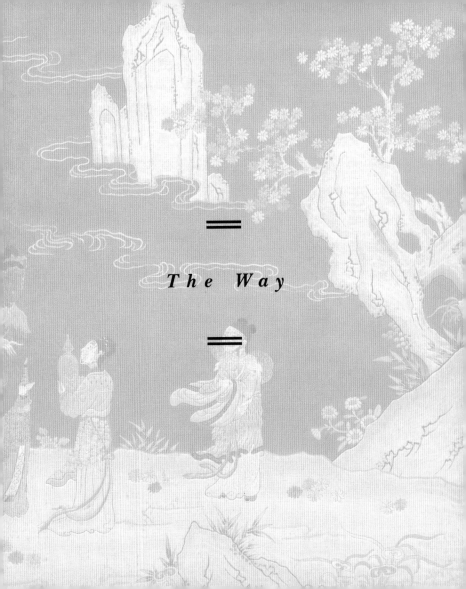

≡

The Way

≡

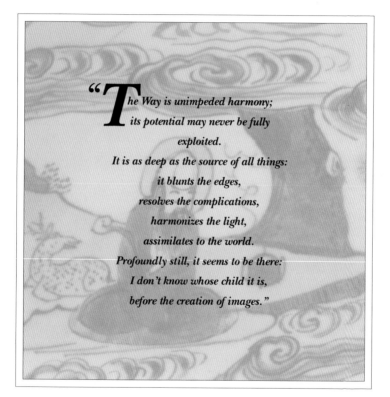

"*The Way is unimpeded harmony;*
its potential may never be fully
exploited.
It is as deep as the source of all things:
it blunts the edges,
resolves the complications,
harmonizes the light,
assimilates to the world.
Profoundly still, it seems to be there:
I don't know whose child it is,
before the creation of images."

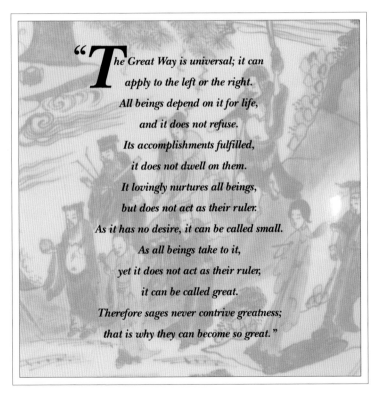

"*The Great Way is universal; it can
apply to the left or the right.
All beings depend on it for life,
and it does not refuse.
Its accomplishments fulfilled,
it does not dwell on them.
It lovingly nurtures all beings,
but does not act as their ruler.
As it has no desire, it can be called small.
As all beings take to it,
yet it does not act as their ruler,
it can be called great.
Therefore sages never contrive greatness;
that is why they can become so great.*"

With all the "verses" in the *Tao Te Ching*, it is ill-advised to comment too closely, for the very isolation of the words, given the concentrated presence of the observer, is essentially enough to grasp the Way implied. We are enjoined towards an acceptance of unim-

peded harmony; that which "allows" nature or God to behave in a way that is perfect already. This applies first to each individual— the concentrated presence—and from there into the "whole way"—the exis-

tence, the universe. We cannot improve, for we *are* it now.

The word Tao suggests a path to be followed, and, by extension, a moral guidance and a code of behavior. Tao has acquired quite different connotations with the passing of time. In the terminology of religion and

magic, it designates the art of establishing communication between Heaven and Earth, between gods and men. Tao in this sense is at once an art, a method, and a power.

Previous pages, 34-35, background image in box: A Chinese dish portraying immortals visiting Shou-lao, God of Longevity. *Above:* A *ruyi,* or Chinese sceptre, carved from light tawny bamboo, with the handle in the form of a branch from which grow foliage and fruits. *Opposite:* T'ien Kuan, a Taoist divinity believed to be the master of Heaven.

This power is seen as a virtue, Te, through which one can bring back the original order both to oneself and to the outside world.

In this way, the Tao is perhaps the most comprehensive symbol in the Chinese language, and with the popularization of the *Tao Te Ching* throughout the world, it has become the symbolic center of the expression of spirituality. All the different ramifications of the word Tao are but symbols of the structure and reality of existence itself. Taoism is thus based on the experience (Lao-tzu himself never speaks of religion) of this universal Way, and Taoists can observe the workings of the Way in the patterns of events taking place in the natural world, in the social world, and in the inner world of the human psyche.

Return To The Origin

In order to recognize the Law of Tao within and outside of ourselves, in the world and in nature, the individual must abandon all ideas that have been imposed from the outside and return instead to the original nature. According to the teachings of Lao-tzu, our inner nature is an extension of the nature of the universe; to follow one is to be in harmony with the other.

To follow nature means being able to accept her support and her cruelty as one state, undivided. Gentle rains or

"Put away holiness, throw away knowledge:
thus the people will profit a hundredfold.
Put away morality, throw away duty:
thus the people will return to filial duty and love.
Put away skillfulness, throw away gain,
and there will no longer be thieves and robbers..."

spring floods, the havoc of a landslide or the beauty of mountain mists—all are part of the whole to which the Sage himself belongs. This natural order was held in classical Chinese thinking to be observable in the regular alternation of the seasons and of night and day. This cycle of hot and cold, light and darkness, is said to reflect the alternating influence of the two sexual principles: Yin and Yang, which governs the behavior of all beings. The Yin, principle of darkness, cold and femininity, invites withdrawal, rest, and

Page 38: Chinese porcelain dish portraying the Taoist divinity Hsi Wang Mu walking on the sea.

passivity. The Yang, principle of light, heat, and masculinity, incites expansion, activity, even aggression. The understanding of Yin and Yang as polarities of oneness is the realization of the Tao.

"If all on earth acknowledge the beautiful as beautiful
then thereby the ugly is already posited.
If all on earth acknowledge the good as good
then thereby is the non-good already posited.
For existence and non-existence generate each other.
Heavy and light complete each other.
Long and short shape each other.
High and deep convert each other.

...In these three things beautiful appearance is not enough.
Therefore take care that men have something to hold on to.
Show simplicity, hold fast to honesty!
Diminish selfishness, reduce desire!
Give up learnedness!
Thus you shall become free of sorrows."

Before and after follow each other.

Thus also is the Man of Calling.
He dwells in effectiveness without action.
He practises teaching without talking.
All beings emerge
and he does not refuse himself to them.
He generates and yet possesses nothing.
He is effective and keeps nothing.
When the work is done
he does not dwell with it.
And just because he does not dwell
he remains undeserted."

All life is governed by the same permanent law: the return to the origin. To know this law is to possess a superior intelligence that Lao-tzu calls "Light," *Ming* in Chinese. However, the Holy Man is not content with just knowing this law intellectually. He seeks to realize it within himself by returning to the Tao in person. The import of this returning is spiritual; it is a matter of identifying himself with the Tao through an inward realization of its unity, simplicity, and emptiness.

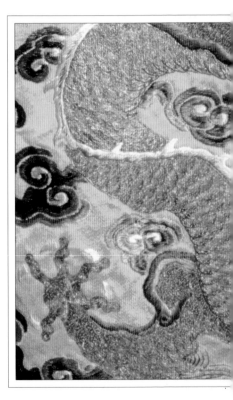

Opposite: A detail from a silk robe portrays a dragon, the Chinese symbol of power.
Overleaf, pages 44-45: Sages using the yin-yang system of divination.

The Void

Within the most ancient of Hindu philosophies the concept of the Void is an intrinsic presence, or lack of presence. For the Hindus and then, as a derivative, the Buddhists, the Void signified absolute nothingness; a beginningless beginning in which literally nothing existed. Consciousness occurred spontaneously when there was a ripple in the Void. Consciousness then gave birth to the dream of mankind. For the Tao, the Void evoked a nothingness, or an emptiness. Lao-tzu's teaching includes a presence which he calls the Void. It is only with an empty heart that one can comprehend the great truths; that which is void is filled by the mystery and wisdom of existence. We can see this exemplified in a number of the expressions within the *Tao Te Ching*:

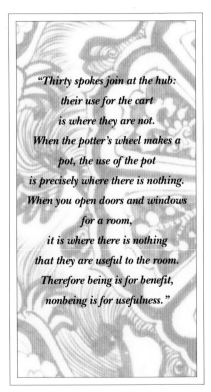

"Thirty spokes join at the hub:
their use for the cart
is where they are not.
When the potter's wheel makes a
pot, the use of the pot
is precisely where there is nothing.
When you open doors and windows
for a room,
it is where there is nothing
that they are useful to the room.
Therefore being is for benefit,
nonbeing is for usefulness."

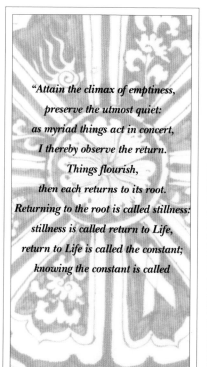

"Attain the climax of emptiness,
preserve the utmost quiet:
as myriad things act in concert,
I thereby observe the return.
Things flourish,
then each returns to its root.
Returning to the root is called stillness:
stillness is called return to Life,
return to Life is called the constant;
knowing the constant is called

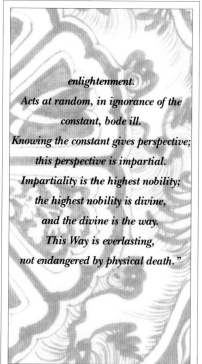

enlightenment.
Acts at random, in ignorance of the
constant, bode ill.
Knowing the constant gives perspective;
this perspective is impartial.
Impartiality is the highest nobility;
the highest nobility is divine,
and the divine is the way.
This Way is everlasting,
not endangered by physical death."

The most exciting and enlightening aspect of each of the "verses" that make up the *Tao Te Ching* is their wholeness. In reading the verses, one takes a journey that is essentially circular in form, traveling on a path that begins somewhere in the middle and ends, again, in the middle, leaving the concentrated presence of the reader replete from a total experience.

When the individual follows the Way he becomes naturally empty. He does not live directly, but "lets himself be lived" by existence. That is why Lao-tzu insists on non-doing, which is not idle inertia, but a total receptiveness to that which wells up from within the heart of hearts. This place within the individual is in communion with and one with existence. This state, "the stateless state," is often described by Lao-tzu as female, as purely receptive. Always we find that same theme—don't force, be natural and in harmony.

Previous pages, 46-47, background image in boxes: A blue and white Yuan Dynasty dish. *Opposite:* A peachbloom, blue and white mallet-shaped dish. *Overleaf, pages 48-49:* A detail from a jade vase.

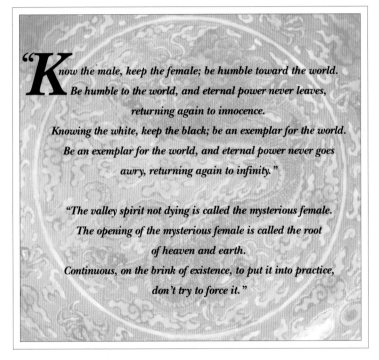

"**K**now the male, keep the female; be humble toward the world.
Be humble to the world, and eternal power never leaves,
returning again to innocence.
Knowing the white, keep the black; be an exemplar for the world.
Be an exemplar for the world, and eternal power never goes
awry, returning again to infinity."

"The valley spirit not dying is called the mysterious female.
The opening of the mysterious female is called the root
of heaven and earth.
Continuous, on the brink of existence, to put it into practice,
don't try to force it."

The Te

he *Tao Te Ching* may be divided into two different sections: the Tao, or exposure of the Way; and the Te, or Virtue, the embodiment of the Tao which enables mankind to accomplish actions within the order of existence.

The man who embodies the Tao, the ideal man, is called "Sheng Ren" throughout the *Tao Te Ching*. One translation of this term is the "Man of Calling," who seeks no benefit for himself, who strives to unite his individual inclinations and wishes, with the Way. The Man of Calling is the embodiment of a cosmic power which governs all things, and is thus immensely powerful himself, albeit not in the conventional way known to the West. Lao-tzu explains this power:

"Skilled warriors of old were subtle,
mysteriously powerful,
so deep they were unknowable.
Just because they are unknowable,
I will try to describe them.
Their wariness was as that of one crossing a river in winter,
their caution was as that of one in fear of all around;
their gravity was as that of a guest,

Above: A porcelain dish painted in blue and enamel colors shows Fu, Lu, and Shou, the three Taoist Gods of Good Fortune. *Opposite:* Ancient Taoist rooftop on the Silk Road in China.

their relaxation was as that of ice at the
melting point.
Simple as uncarved wood,
open as the valleys,
they were inscrutable as murky water.
Who can, in turbidity,
use the gradual clarification of stillness?

Who can, long at rest,
use the gradual enlivening of movement?
Those who preserve this Way do not want
fullness.
Just because of not wanting fullness,
it is possible to use to the full and not make
anew."

The Tao In Practice

In practice as in philosophy of the Tao, there is no 'yes' and 'no':

"Chao-chou asked Nan-ch'uan, 'What is the Tao?' Nan-ch'uan said, 'Everyday mind is the Tao.'

Chao-chou said, 'How can I approach it?' Nan-ch'uan said, 'The more you try to approach it, the farther away you'll be.'

'But if I don't get close, how can I understand it?'

The Master said, 'It's not a question of understanding or not understanding.

Understanding is delusion; not understanding is indifference. But when you reach the unattainable Tao, it is like pure space, limitless and serene. Where is there room in it for yes or no?'"

The Tao, later called Taoism, eventually transformed into an organized religious structure composed of monasteries, temples, images, liturgies, and rites, due to the efforts of Chang Tao-ling.

Chang Tao-ling was known to posterity as the "Heavenly Teacher" who supposedly started his work in the 1st or 2nd century A.D. In turn, each of his pupils succeeded him to

Page 54: Entrance to a Taoist temple.
Above: Joss sticks burning at the gates of a Taoist shrine. *Opposite:* A gilt bronze incense burner from the Tang Dynasty.

the name Chang, "Heavenly Teacher," until the present. This tradition has continued even beyond the end of Taoism as an officially recognized religion, which coincided with the founding of the Chinese Republic.

Living in harmony with nature's rhythms, the essence of the teaching of Lao-tzu, is today a highly regarded virtue, and more and more people are choosing the positive attitudes of the Tao to cope with the problems they and the world face. The *Tao Te Ching* is currently one of the widest read Eastern religious texts, and the Tao is practiced all over the world in a variety of forms and applications: Taoist yoga, yoga meaning "union" in Sanskrit; Taoist horticulture, avoiding artificiality in the care of plants; Taoist meditation and breathing, helping to achieve the stillness of our original nature; Taoist art; and Taoist education. But above all, the Tao remains a method of gaining personal and collective wisdom to understand and preserve the nature of all things, a method that could happily be learned in the Western civilized world where an acceptance of nature is still far from present.

BIBLIOGRAPHY

John Blofeld, *Beyond the Gods - Taoist and Buddhist Mysticism,* George Allen & Unwin Ltd., London, 1974

John Blofeld, *The Secret and the Sublime - Taoist Mysteries and Magic,* George Allen & Unwin Ltd., London, 1973

Thomas Cleary, *The Essential Tao,* HarperSanFrancisco, San Francisco, 1991

Max Kaltenmark, *Lao Tzu and Taoism, translated from the French by Roger Greaves,* Stanford University Press, Stanford, California, 1969

Lao Tzu, *Tao Te Ching, The Richard Wilhelm Edition,* Arkana, Penguin Books Ltd., London, 1990

Holmes Welch, *The Parting of the Way - Lao Tzu and the Taoist Movement,* Methuen and Co. Ltd., London, 1958

Graham, A.C., *Chung Tzu: The Inner Chapters,* George Allen and Unwin, London, 1981, 1986
The Book of Lieh-tzu, Columbia University Press, New York, 1990

Henricks, Robert G., *Lao-tzu Te-tao Ching: A New Translation Based on the Recently Discovered Ma-wang-tui Texts,* Ballantine, New York, 1992

LaFargue, Roger, *The Tao of the Tao-te Ching,* State University of New York, 1992

Lau, D.C., *Lao Tzu: Tao Te Ching,* Penguin Books, Baltimore, 1963

Mitchell, Stephen, *Tao Te Ching,* A New English Version, Harper & Row, Publishers, New York, 1988

While every effort has been made to trace all present copyright holders of the material in this book, whether companies or individuals, any unintentional omission is hereby apologized for in advance and we will be pleased to correct any errors in acknowledgments in any future edition of this book.

Text acknowledgments:

pp. 20–21, 40–41 — Excerpts from *Tao Te Ching by Lao Tzu, The Richard Wilhelm Edition,* translated into English by H. G. Ostwold, (Arkana, London, 1990), English translation copyright © 1985 by Routledge & Kegan Paul. Reproduced by permission of Penguin Books Ltd.

pp. 28–29, 30, 34, 35, 46, 47, 49, 52–53 — Excerpts from *The Essential Tao* by Thomas Cleary. Copyright © 1991 by Thomas Cleary. Reproduced by permission of HarperCollins Publishers.

Picture acknowledgments:

Courtesy of the Trustees of the Victoria & Albert Museum; Pages: 7, 10, 28, 30, 32, 36.
Christies Images; Pages: 12, 14, 17, 22, 46, 48, 49, 50, 57.
Ancient Art and Architecture Collection, London; Pages: 8, 18, 27, 43, 53.
CM Dixon; Pages: 23, 24, 31, 34, 37, 38, 44, 52.
Circa Photo Library; Pages: 4, 54, 56, 58.

Jacket: *Ancient Art & Architecture, Christies' Images, CM Dixon, Circa Photo Library.*